Springs of Hope

Meditations of the Heart

Marilee Donivan

Simple Faith Books
Boise, Idaho

SPRINGS OF HOPE: Meditations of the Heart
© Copyright 2013
Marilee Donivan
All rights reserved

Unless otherwise identified, all Scripture quotations are taken from the NEW AMERICAN STANDARD BIBLE®, Copyright ©1960, 1962, 1963,1968, 1971,1972,1973,1975,1977,1995 by The Lockman Foundation. Used by permission.
Scripture quotations marked (NIV) are taken from HOLY BIBLE, NEW INTERNATIONAL VERSION®. Copyright ©1973, 1978, 1984 by International Bible Society. Used by permission of Zondervan Publishing House. All rights reserved.
Scripture quotations (AMP) are taken from The Amplified Bible, Old Testament copyright © 1965, 1987 by the Zondervan Corporation and The Amplified New Testament copyright © 1958, 1987 by The Lockman Foundation. Used by permission. All rights reserved.
Scripture quotations (KJV) are taken from The Holy Bible, Authorized King James Version, New Scofield Reference Bible. Copyright ©1967.
Scripture quotations marked (NLT) are taken from Holy Bible. New Living Translation copyright© 1996, 2004, 2007 by Tyndale House Foundation. Used by permission of Tyndale House Publishers Inc., Carol Stream, Illinois 60188. All rights reserved.
Scripture quotations marked (NKJV) are taken fromThe Holy Bible, New King James Version Copyright © 1982 by Thomas Nelson, Inc.

Text copyright © 2013 Marilee Donivan. All rights reserved.
Illustrations copyright © 2013 Marilee Donivan, "You Can Do It! ART" All rights reserved.
Cover painting copyright © 2013 Marilee Donivan. All rights reserved
Cover and interior design by Marilee Donivan
www.SunriseMountainBooks.com

v.1.0

ISBN : 978-0-9842362-7-5

This book may not be reproduced, transmitted, or stored in whole or in part by any means, including graphic, electronic, or mechanical, without the express written consent of the publisher, except in the case of brief quotations embodied in critical articles and reviews.

Published by Simple Faith Books,
a division of Sunrise Mountain Books
13347 W. Tapatio Drive
Boise, ID 83713

PRINTED IN THE UNITED STATES OF AMERICA

Dedication

To Tom,
My Joy,
Strong Encourager,
And Gentle Advisor

PREFACE

Overwhelmed. Exhausted. Stressed. Sleepless. Consumed with worry. These expressions are all too common in our daily conversations! It's not the conversation that is distressing; it's the bombardment of busyness and burden-bearing that is our trouble. Obviously, we are in desperate need of hope, refreshment, and rest.

I have been through my own series of "wilderness experiences" from various circumstances and unplanned events, so the thoughts expressed in this book are personal and authentic, not theoretical hypothesizing. I am currently enjoying precious refreshment even in the midst of a busy season of life and it's my hope and prayer that these thoughts from my own experiences, sharing the incomparable Word of God, will encourage and revitalize you, my fellow traveler, as they have me.

Because I find my thoughts relax and flow with the watercolors I paint with, I've combined that pleasure with reflections on some of my favorite scriptures. I hope you'll enjoy browsing the artwork and will find your imagination and memories stirred through the colors and shapes, giving you a mini-vacation whenever you pick up the book. I'm with you on the journey and pray that you will be blessed by God's comfort, encouragement, and inspiration as you take a break and spend a little time of rest and renewal wherever you are.

With you on the journey,

Marilee Donivan

SINGING PRAISES

"Praise the Lord! Praise God in his sanctuary; praise Him in his mighty expanse. Praise Him for His mighty deeds; Praise Him according to His excellent greatness. Praise Him with trumpet sound; Praise Him with harp and lyre. Praise Him with timbrel and dancing; Praise Him with stringed instruments and pipe. Praise Him with loud cymbals; Praise Him with resounding cymbals. Let everything that has breath praise the Lord. Praise the Lord!" Psalm 150

When I reflect on the great and mighty things God has done to show His strength and power, I am filled with joy. It is awe-inspiring to recall the ways He has shown His love in countless answered prayers. Why do I think today will be any different? I want to remember His goodness and His power during the day as I go about my tasks. Yet, I find I am easily distracted and sometimes overwhelmed by problems that I don't have immediate solutions for. How helpful it is to remind myself that God is never inattentive! The Lord reigns in His glorious majesty, always working mightily on behalf of those who trust Him, whose hearts are turned toward Him. I wait expectantly for yet another display of His excellency.

Music, whether from harp, piano, trumpet, cymbals, or flute, brings forth expressions of the heart. The production of music somehow lifts my attitude and emotions above the ordinary. Artistic painting does the same thing for me. Even painting the walls of my home! Goodness, even cleaning a closet produces a feeling of contentment. There is something wonderful about creating something that is right and new, and that is what God does beyond measure. He makes all things new, surprisingly, joyfully, magnificently new. New attitudes, new perspectives, new experiences. Nothing is too hard for Him. He does all things well. Oh, how I praise Him for His excellent ways, His beauty and perfection!

God is already at work to bring blessings to you. There is an invisible realm that is very real, and you are part of that picture, a recipient of God's love and grace. Just as the apostle Paul said, "I am confident of this very thing, that He who began a good work in you will perfect it until the day of Jesus Christ" (Philippians 1:6 NASB).

Thank You, Lord, for promising completion of Your continuing work in me. There is so much to be done! Thank You that You know how to make it happen! I praise You for Your patience and power. Help me to praise You not only with my voice and my music, but also with my thoughts, my attitudes, and in all that I do.

GOD LOVES SURPRISES

"For My thoughts are not your thoughts, nor are your ways My ways," declares the Lord. For as the heavens are higher than the earth, so are My ways higher than your ways and My thoughts than your thoughts. For as the rain and the snow come down from heaven, and do not return there without watering the earth and making it bear and sprout, and furnishing seed to the sower and bread to the eater, so will My word be which goes forth from My mouth; it will not return to Me empty, without accomplishing what I desire, and without succeeding in the matter for which I sent it. For you will go out with joy and be led forth with peace; The mountains and the hills will break forth into shouts of joy before you, and all the trees of the field will clap their hands." Isaiah 55:8-12

God's ways are so beyond what I can imagine. He constantly surprises me! And I love it that way. I'm so glad He isn't limited to my imagination! The anticipated surprises keep me on my toes, like a child looking through a store window to see things that are new, perhaps never even dreamed of.

I have now lived more years than I have left to live on this earth. I think being in the second half of life is actually an advantage when it comes to exercising faith. I now have a wonderful memory log of the amazing things God has shown me over the years, in the ways He came up with answers to my perplexing questions and what seemed to be impossible problems to solve. So, now I have stopped trying to figure out everything ahead of time; I just pray and take the next step that seems appropriate and good. And then watch day by day to see what develops, with a willingness to adjust my actions according to what new thing God may show me.

Even the mountains, the hills, and the trees celebrate God's faithfulness. I love seeing the breeze dance through the branches of trees, especially the quaking aspens that surrounded my home some years ago. The leaves looked and sounded like joyful clapping hands, and reminded me that God's faithful watchfulness and love would bring forth exactly what was needed to accomplish His will for my life.

When I need a spiritual shot in the arm, I take time to observe the natural world, to let its beauty and intricacy speak to me of the power that created them.

Thank You, Lord, for the good and beautiful things to come! Everything You plan will come to pass, and Your ways are higher and better than my own. Thank You! I join the chorus of all Your creation to praise You for who You are and the indescribable blessing of knowing You.

DEFEATING FALSE GUILT

"I will bring the blind by a way they did not know; I will lead them in paths they have not known. I will make darkness light before them, and crooked places straight. These are the things I will do; I will not forsake them." Isaiah 42:16-17 (NKJV)

Sometimes our paths are not straight, but are crooked, twisted, winding, taking us places we later may have regrets about. We cannot get a do-over; they happened and are part of our history. The important thing is to leave those regrettable events as history and not allow them to become current news to review daily at the breakfast table. *"As far as the east is from the west, so far have I removed your transgressions from you," says the Lord. (Psalm 103:12)* If we believe Him, there is no room for self-condemnation. "I know," you say, "but I can't forgive myself." I battled this for several years until the day I realized my terrible error. Illuminating thoughts put me back on track: Am I more important than God? Is my point of view more valid than His? When I reject the right to be free of guilt and condemnation, to walk in forgiveness, aren't I insisting my judgment carries more weight than God's? Dangerous, subtle deception! If God calls me forgiven, it is my arrogant pride that says His forgiveness is not sufficient to free me from wallowing in guilt and regret.

The enemy of our souls, the devil, will accuse and emphasize our past errors and will beat us down with reoccurring condemnation; because if we continue in defeat with a self-condemning attitude, then the cross of Christ appears to have had no effect for us. And Satan achieves a temporary win.

Satan doesn't let go of such things easily, but in Christ we are victorious and have all authority over the enemy. I speak the truth out loud whenever false guilt comes upon me, and eventually the light and truth of God's Word defeats the accuser. It always does.

God wants us free. Use God's holy and eternal Word. Speak the truth boldly: "I am forgiven in Christ! Therefore there is now NO condemnation to those who are in Christ Jesus!" (Romans 8:1) By and by, the false accusations of guilt and condemnation will lose their grip, truth will take its place, and you will enjoy the freedom and abundant life Jesus Christ bought for you with His precious blood.

Thank You, O God, for setting captives free! Help me realize my freedom from condemnation and live the abundant life You have given me as Your forgiven child.

GOD WITH US

"On the glorious splendor of Your majesty and on Your wonderful works, I will meditate." Psalm 145:5

God has made Himself known to us. What a stunning reality! The Bible tells of His interactions with men, women, kings, children, prophets, the faithful and unfaithful. He has not hidden Himself from us. The greatest display of His Being was through His Son, Jesus Christ. Jesus was called Emmanuel, meaning *God with us*. We are without excuse if we say we cannot know God. Even all of creation shows His power and presence. I am amazed when I spend time meditating on who God is in all His majesty, glory, complexity, and power. I am in total awe that the magnificent Most High God wants us to know Him because He desires relationship with us.

God had choices. He could have chosen to put us on this planet, leaving us alone to stumble and bumble our way from birth to extinction. Instead, He graciously chose to reveal His love and majesty through His creation and His personal interactions in our lives.

I have choices, too. I can choose to go through life on my own steam, relying on my own efforts and experiences. Or I can choose to ask for help. It's hard to ask for help! Self-sufficiency is applauded in our culture, and we succumb to the idea that the more self-sufficient we are, the more successful we are. Pride fuels the deception. The Bible tells us God is the "helper of the helpless," and "a very present help in time of trouble." I have a choice to believe what others tell me, or to believe what God says. I must sort through the voices and decide which ones are true and will have pre-eminence. Jesus spoke of having eyes to see, ears to hear, and hearts to understand. Not all I see, hear, or think I understand is solidly correct, and should be carefully weighed before I agree to it and adopt it as my own.

Thankfully, we are not on our own. The meaning of Emmanuel takes on grand significance. God *with us*! We have the Holy Spirit to guide our thoughts and illuminate our perceptions. We have God's holy Word to instruct and correct us. We have His awesome power at work in us, and His willingness to bring forth amazing transformations. He is limited by nothing and is motivated by His inexhaustible love.

Loving Father, give me wisdom today to remember how great You are and how great Your love is for us. Help me to be humble and to bring my needs to You, ready to receive the help You are so ready to give. Thank You that You are not only the Mighty God of splendor, majesty and power; You are also my wise Teacher, patient Comforter, gentle Shepherd, and faithful Provider.

STAYING PLANTED

"Blessed is the one... whose delight is in the law of the Lord, and in His law he meditates day and night. He will be like a tree firmly planted by streams of water which yields its fruit in its season and its leaf does not wither; And in whatever he does, he prospers." Psalm 1:1-3

Delighting in God's law and meditating in it day and night. Truly, over the years, my love for God's Word has grown, and now is such a part of me that throughout the day and in wakeful night hours, I contemplate it in light of all kinds of people and events capturing my attention. His Word gives me truth in the midst of confusion, instruction for challenges, reassurance and comfort during grief, loss, disappointment, and disillusionment. I treasure its power to transform my thinking, words, and actions.

Thank you, Lord, for planting me beside your streams of living water where I can drink in the unending supply of your Word. You've given me roots of stability in uncertain times. I marvel that even now, after reading your Word for more than 40 years, its power and supply is never exhausted. Like your mercy and love, it is new every morning.

"You lead me beside still waters." "You *make* me lie down in green pastures." "You restore my soul." (Psalm 23) I enjoy the peace You bring when You have *made* me lie down. I didn't want to lie down—I wanted to keep going, going, going, thinking I had to accomplish something, that my purpose was to achieve a particular goal. But, when You *made* me lie down, You showed me that I most needed Your peace, reassurance, and time with You. I'm so thankful for the times You've overruled my desires and plans and provided Your much better plan for me—to enjoy You.

It amazes me that it pleases You to have the attention of Your children so much that You will cause a pause! You put us in a position where we finally *must* lay down our tools and strategies and grandiose plans. You quiet us and gently whisper, "Listen. Listen."

Oh, the wondrous things I have heard You say when I am finally listening! You place quiet but undeniable impressions upon my heart. Lord, please keep me planted, listening, and thirsty for Your Word.

"Be merciful to me, O God, be merciful to me! For my soul trusts in You;
And in the shadow of Your wings I will make my refuge until these calamities have passed by.

"I will cry out to God Most High, to God who performs all things for me.

"He shall send from heaven and save me; He reproaches the one who would swallow me up. Selah. God shall send forth His mercy and His truth." Psalm 57:1-3 (NKJV)

"On my bed I remember you; I think of you through the watches of the night.

"Because you are my help, I sing in the shadow of your wings.

"I cling to you; your right hand upholds me." Psalm 63:6-8 (NIV)

UNDER HIS WINGS

There have been times in my life I have just wanted to run and hide! If I were a child, you would find me under the bed, or in a closet corner, crouching behind long hanging dresses. I felt safe there. It was dark and quiet, and it was my self-designated "time out" before the term became fashionable. The closet is no longer exactly appropriate. So now I have found a new "closet" space. God's Word paints a memorable picture of a better hiding place—under His wings. What better place could there be than the comforting, soft, warm presence of great protective wings spread over my trembling soul!

Jesus used the same striking analogy as He grieved for Jerusalem shortly before He submitted to the cross. *"Jerusalem, Jerusalem, who kills the prophets, and stones those who are sent to her! How often I wanted to gather your children together, the way a hen gathers her chicks under her wings, and you were unwilling." Matthew 23:37 (NASB)* It's a tender picture of God's expansive love, inclusive even of those who reject Him. How much comfort we can take, knowing God's all-encompassing "wings" are always spread over us in times of distress.

Thank You, Lord, for word pictures like these, which stay with me in dark hours. Sometimes I don't have words to express my frayed emotions and confusing thoughts; but in my mind's eye I see myself tucked tenderly under Your wings until all my fears and concerns subside. Your Word is truth, and I am safe with You.

DANCING AGAIN

"You have turned my mourning into joyful dancing. You have taken away my clothes of mourning and clothed me with joy, that I might sing praises to you and not be silent. O Lord my God, I will give you thanks forever!" Psalm 30:11-12 (NLT)

We never know what joys await us around the corner of our misery. During tough times, joy seems so very far away and out of reach. It is impossible to imagine the relief, but hold on! God rewards faith. And He is not limited to the best that we can dream up. He is able to do above and beyond all that we can ask or think (Ephesians 3:20) and He is pleased to make it happen! Don't look at what He has done for others, for His super-abundant provision will be tailor-made specifically for you. He knows what you need and what you desire.

"Though it tarries, wait." Habakkuk 2:3 encourages us to wait. *"For the vision is yet for an appointed time and it hastens to the end [fulfillment]; it will not deceive or disappoint. Though it tarry, wait [earnestly] for it, because it will surely come; it will not be behindhand on its appointed day. (AMP)*

God mercifully prepares an appointed time when the trial will subside. I'll be honest. It's never as soon as I desire. But with hindsight (sometimes quite a while later), I ultimately agree with God that He was not late at all with His answers. Though it is miserable to wait, when relief comes after a prolonged wait, I appreciate God's grace and power all the more. Raising children provides us good examples of the wisdom of withholding or delaying certain results, versus instant gratification, which too often produces demanding greed and unappreciative selfishness. How good it is to see a child hope, wait, and trust his parent to provide, though the wait is a long one. Don't we love to see a child's joy when we produce the reward after great patience!

I remind myself that beautiful music is composed of notes, rhythms, and rests. The musical pauses, rests, add as much to the beauty as the notes.

Our wise, sovereign God knows what will bless you like nothing else will. Trust Him. Though it is hard to wait, tune your ears to the small joys you detect in your day while you wait for the grand crescendo that is to come. You will not be disappointed. You'll be dancing during the grand finale!

Thank You, Lord, for the wait, the rewards, music, and rests.

BREAKFAST OF CHAMPIONS

"The faithful love of the Lord never ends! His mercies never cease. Great is his faithfulness; his mercies begin afresh each morning. I say to myself, 'The Lord is my inheritance; therefore, I will hope in him'!" Lamentations 3:22-24 (NLT)

I love mornings. To me, they are a promise of new things, like an unopened gift that has some wonderful item inside to put to use, or to enjoy as a lovely remembrance of the sweet giver. When I open my eyes in the morning, I deliberately put behind me the events of the day before, and feel I have a fresh start at whatever challenge I faced through the night or previous days. Who doesn't love a fresh beginning after a trying time?

I don't take sufficient rest periods when I am working to solve a problem or learning a new task. I can drive people crazy with my sighs of exasperation when I'm in the midst of a steep learning curve. Perseverance is a virtue; but my tenacity tends to slide over into obsession when I become determined to force my way through an unyielding roadblock. I don't seem to learn from past experiences, which have shown me that if I will just leave the project for a while—perhaps a few minutes, or hours, or overnight—I will return to it with a sudden "aha" realization of where I was missing it. And the fix becomes doable.

In my obstinancy, I fail to remember that we are wired for rhythms of work and rest. My error is, "When I get *just this one more* piece completed, *then* I will rest." God tells us to take time to rest. I am far more successful when I finally do that.

Along with physical rest from tasks, spiritual rest is important to our good mental health. "Labor, therefore, to enter into that spiritual rest," (Hebrews 4:11). Sounds like a riddle to "labor to enter into rest." But, when I relax and give my attention to spiritual truths, reading in God's Word and meditating on its meaning, my soul breathes a deep, satisfied sigh, and my body, soul, and spirit feel refreshed.

Thank You, Lord, for Your mercies. What a gift You give, allowing me to begin anew each morning. Help me to leave yesterday behind and look forward to the blessings You will send me today.

SUNSET CHASERS

"I will thank you, Lord, among all the people. I will sing your praises among the nations. For your unfailing love is higher than the heavens. Your faithfulness reaches to the clouds. Be exalted, O God, above the highest heavens; May your glory shine over all the earth." Psalm 108:3-5 (NLT)
"Blessed be the name of the Lord from this time forth and forever. From the rising of the sun to its setting, the name of the Lord is to be praised.
The Lord is high above all nations; His glory is above the heavens." Psalm 114:2-4

My son and daughter-in-law have an insatiable appreciation of sunsets. When they lived in the same town as I, I would sometimes get a call from them, "Have you seen the sunset? You need to go outside right now!" It was fun to share the light, colors, and shadows in the sky with them as we "oohed and aahed" together over a glorious finish to the day. They lived 20 miles across town, but we all saw the same magnificent display stretching from a brilliant horizon into the darkening purple expanse of the unsearchable universe overhead. One by one, stars sprinkled the spaces. It was always a touching reminder to me that God's love also spanned the miles between us, and He was as accessible to me as He was to them at any given moment. His same glorious power and love reaches out to all of us, no matter how far away we are from one another. It is a wonder.

At such times, regardless of all the day has included—the good, the bad, and the ugly—the heavenly panorama declares God's beauty. His faithfulness in keeping the sun and stars in place, Earth's incessant orbit, and the rhythm of each 24-hour gift, continues to remind me of His unfailing love. Praise bubbles up in my heart, and joy replaces the disappointments that may have stolen peace from me during the midday hours.

Lord God, Master Designer, Your beauty surrounds me every day. Thank You for daily reminders that You are always accessible. Help me to see Your beauty in everyday things, that I may be encouraged at the end of the day and trust You more for each tomorrow.

SONGS IN THE NIGHT

"He heals the brokenhearted and binds up their wounds. He determines the number of the stars and calls them each by name. Great is our Lord and mighty in power; his understanding has no limit." Psalm 147:3-5 (NIV)
"I remembered my songs in the night." Psalm 77:6 (NIV)
"He will quiet you with His love; He will rejoice over you with singing." Zephaniah 3:17

What a glorious thought! God, who made the heavens and the earth and all that is in them—this powerful Creator—watches over us while we sleep! He calls all the stars by name—such an uncountable vastness! He surely must know my name, too, for there are infinitely more stars in the vast universe than there are people on earth.

At times, it's hard to appreciate that we are personally known by God. Times of worry, strain, and troubles lure us to think He's not paying attention. Yet, He sees us and He understands our weaknesses, even our erroneous and doubting thoughts.

During a prolonged time of waiting for God to break through to bring healing in a desperate time, I was comforted by songs that came to me during many wakeful nights. They were songs of hope and faith I had learned earlier in my Christian life, and they "visited" me sometimes even during sleep. It was sweet to wake up with a song somehow already singing in my mind even before I was fully conscious of the new morning. At odd times during the day, songs like "Blessed Assurance," "Our God is an Awesome God," "No, Never Alone," "'Tis so Sweet to Trust in Jesus," and many others were tremendous reassurances that God had been with me through the dark hours of the night and was with me still as I met the new day.

Bolstered by these encouraging experiences, I now ask God to give me songs and words of inspiration as I sleep. I need His constant inflow of faith, hope, and strengthening; and I love that He provides these even in the nighttime when we are not consciously aware of it.

Thank You, Lord, for renewing my mind and body in surprising ways with Your perfect bedside manner.

PRACTICING STILLNESS

"Be still and know that I am God. I will be exalted among the nations, I will be exalted in the earth!" Psalm 46:10 (AMP)
"He leads me beside the still and restful waters." Psalm 23:2 (AMP)
"In returning [to Me] and resting [in Me] you shall be saved; in quietness and in [trusting] confidence shall be your strength." Isaiah 30:15 (AMP)

I've noticed it is often hard to find a place of stillness. It's almost foreign to our culture. Offices, businesses, gyms, restaurants, restrooms, shopping malls, medical facilities, waiting rooms all seem to have a constant bombardment of noise! Perhaps it's a news channel or a talk show, or a video that is playing. Even if it is music, often it is not the kind of music we would choose. Somehow the idea that we need to be entertained at all times has become the norm. It is now so common to most spaces that what we really notice is walking into a room with an *absence* of sound! We wonder if everything is alright and glance around nervously to see if anyone else notices that it's *quiet!*

I've almost forgotten how to clear my mind of the noisy clutter, find a quiet spot, and think my own thoughts. No wonder God finds it necessary to instruct us, "Be still."

What happens when we are still? Our bodies relax, our stress level drops, and we have time to sort through all the varied influences that are fighting for space in our mind and emotions. We can set aside the unimportant and spend time prioritizing the unending lists of things we think we need to be doing. We can even decide *not* to think about lists or priorities, and just *rest!* This, God tells us through Isaiah, is where we renew our strength and find salvation. God says to return to Him and rest in Him! We find strength in our quiet moments of deliberately realigning our thoughts to trustfully place our confidence in God. I feel better already, just reminding myself that this is available to me right now!

It's hard to feel confident when our minds are whirling with indecision and overloaded thoughts. Confidence is restored when I take time to realize what is true and Who is on my side. "If God is for us, who can be against us?" (Romans 8:31 NKJV) God is for us! Like David against Goliath, God-confidence overcomes my tendency to hurry, worry, and panic.

Thank You, Lord, for being my rest, my strength, and my confidence. Remind me to slow down so I can enjoy the peace you offer me.

GRACE AND GLORY

*"The Lord is my light and my salvation; whom shall I fear?" Psalm 27:1-7
"For the Lord God is a sun and a shield; The Lord will give grace and glory. No good thing will He withhold from them who walk uprightly." Psalm 84:11 (NKJV)*

Fear is an insidious monster. It begins with a suggestion, "What if...?" If I entertain the idea, it grows. It can take on a life of its own, as if it has substance. Our minds handle worries as if they are real, and our bodies react—with tight stomachs, headaches, muscle fatigue, or illness. It's no fun. It takes mental discipline to refuse to entertain worrisome thoughts. They are intrusive and relentless if not dealt a decisive blow with the sword of truth!

Here is truth: "The Lord is a sun" to us. Our sun illuminates and warms, gives life to growing things, and is the essential hub of our solar system. Its radiance is constant; it will not fade. Even during the night, the sun has not ceased to shine; it is only unseen because our global location has turned its back for a few hours.

More truth: "The Lord is a shield" to us. We do not know the number of calamities we are spared because of God's gracious shielding. He is a shield against our spiritual enemies, and shields us from untimely happenings. Although "the rain falls on the just and the unjust," the Lord shields us from things that He knows we absolutely could not bear. (I Corinthians 10:13)

"No good thing will He withhold from them who walk uprightly." I believe this, even though there have been times I have asked for "good things" and they were not granted. Although God has no obligation to explain things to me, He has graciously sometimes allowed me to see with hindsight the wisdom and purpose He exercised when He withheld certain things I desired. I'm so grateful!

Reflecting on specific memories of this heightens my awareness that He sees and knows so much more than I do, and that His withholding is actually exquisite love in action for me.

Thank You, Lord, that You are supremely wise and good in all You do and in all You withhold. Help me to trust You in it all and be thankful that You lovingly shield me from things I have no idea of. Please forgive me for my short-sightedness, and increase my faith.

EMBRACING CHANGE

"Consider the lilies, how they grow: they neither toil nor spin; but I tell you, not even Solomon in all his glory clothed himself like one of these. But if God so clothes the grass in the field, which is alive today and tomorrow is thrown into the furnace, how much more will He clothe you? You men of little faith! And do not seek what you will eat and what you will drink, and do not keep worrying. For all these things the nations of the world eagerly seek; but your Father knows that you need these things. But seek His kingdom, and these things will be added to you. Do not be afraid, little flock, for your Father has chosen gladly to give you the kingdom." Luke 12:28

I love the seasons. I enjoy the changing scenery, weather and colors. The seasons remind me of God's faithful provision for the changing times of my own life. The snows come to beautify the dried grasses and bare limbs of autumn. The crocuses and tulips valiantly pop through the earth to declare they were there all the time, just waiting for their moment to adorn the landscape with new textures, shapes, fragrances, and colors. The warmth of summer brings a sense of growth and discovery, with thriving gardens, active birds, exploring ants, and dancing butterflies. Better weather encourages travel for reconnections with family and friends. Things are always changing.

It is tempting to become anxious in times of change. None of us knows the future. Speculators and pundits warn us of dire events that will surely invade our predictable lives. They could be right. But the Lord Jesus tells us not to be anxious. God, our creator, has our lives on His radar screen. Not only does He know where we are and what lies ahead, He will make provision for it, just as He does for the birds and the flowers in the seasons that unfold year after year.

As new challenges confront us, whether in health, finances, relationships, loss, career changes or any other, God is never caught by surprise! Our greatest challenge will be to stay focused on who God is and what He says about His love for us, His children. I believe as we keep God's Word firmly tucked inside our hearts to draw upon for truth and reassurance, we will see new demonstrations of His power, glory, and provision for the coming times that will excite and energize our walk with Him as never before.

Thank You, Lord, that all the changes in my life are under Your watchful guidance. You care about everything that concerns me.

WATER IN THE DESERT

"For I will pour water on him who is thirsty, and floods on the dry ground; I will pour My Spirit on your descendants, and My blessing on your offspring..." Isaiah 44:3 (NKJV)

"Forget the former things; do not dwell on the past. See, I am doing a new thing! Now it springs up; do you not perceive it? I am making a way in the wilderness and streams in the wasteland." Isaiah 43:18-19 (NIV)

There are many Biblical references to water. They are always deeply significant, often with layers of meaning. Physical bodies of water are life sources. We cannot live long without water. In addition to The Red Sea, the Jordan River, heaven-sent rain, and water from the rock, are Old Testament references to spiritual water giving life, refreshment, and renewal. In the New Testament, Jesus Christ refers to Himself as "living water" which quenches spiritual thirst and satisfies forever. Believers are promised streams of living water to sustain and refresh us on the dusty roads of daily living, and in the severe desert times of our lives when we feel parched and utterly lifeless.

We feel the wilderness heat when we've experienced a series of blows that leave us reeling; when we've battled for what is right and good; when we've failed; when others have turned against us; when we've been betrayed. When we've suffered losses and are trying to recover stability but are staggering and searching for an exit from the fray, we need relief. We need refreshment.

Enter Jesus, offering His cool, clear living water to pour over our wounds and rinse the dirty residue away. God's promises are sure. He will flood us with renewing springs of His living water. He tells us to forget the past; don't dwell there. Look for the new things our Creator God delights in bringing forth. When God makes things new, His timing is perfect. It's real and it's lasting. It's cause for celebration. Be expectant. He is making a way out of the wilderness for you, and is preparing to release His stored-up blessings for you and your offspring!

Lord, please help me to live with an attitude of expectancy, remembering that no wilderness experience is forever. Thank You for Your perfect, refreshing water for my weary body and spirit.

FAITHFUL RHYTHMS

"Now faith is the substance of things hoped for, the evidence of things not seen." Hebrews 11:1 (KJV)
"Now faith is the assurance (the confirmation, the title deed) of the things [we] hope for, being the proof of things [we] do not see and the conviction of their reality [faith perceiving as real fact what is not revealed to the senses]." (AMP)

I watched the echocardiogram monitor with fascination. It revealed the inside of my heart, its chambers, valves, and pulsing activity. Beating, beating, beating, the constancy of the rhythm was almost hypnotic. While the technician checked and measured and objectively recorded, I was mesmerized by what I saw on the screen. The ceaseless heart faithfully pumped life, performing its purposeful duty over and over and over, quietly, without fanfare, as it has been doing for years. This essential on-going task in each of us is usually invisible; we probably even take it for granted while we go about our daily lives. Out of sight, out of mind.

But at this moment in time, it took center stage. My thoughts flew to God, realizing with great clarity and awe that my life was in His hands. It always has been. He is the great controller and sustainer of all life. His intricate design of the heart and its interaction with the rest of the body is a magnificent display of His genius and creativity. I had the startling realization that God is constantly at work in all of my life in the same way. Much of what He is up to is invisible to me; but He is faithfully working behind the scenes to provide the substance of what is required for every aspect of my life. The fact that I cannot see what He is doing doesn't detract from the grand significance of this truth.

My part is to wait and trust in what is yet to come—the unseen. God, who created my heart and yours, keeps them constantly at work, allowing us to live another day to glorify Him by trusting Him for His plan, which absolutely without a doubt will be completed according to the purpose He has lovingly designed for us.

Thank You, O God, that although Your ways are often mysterious, You are ceaselessly working and all things will be knit together for good as I continue to follow You, just as You say in Your Word (Romans 8:28).

FORGET-ME-NOTS

"But Zion said, 'The Lord has forsaken me, and the Lord has forgotten me.' 'Can a woman forget her nursing child and have no compassion on the son of her womb? Even these may forget, but I will not forget you. Behold, I have inscribed you on the palms of My hands...'" Isaiah 49:14-16

    Sometimes after a major loss we feel painfully insignificant and even wonder if there is any purpose remaining for our lives. Accumulating trials and adjustments can accentuate feelings of uncertainty and worthlessness while we struggle to cope.

    I was a recent widow, and beginning a new life with all its adjustments was taking its toll. I was wrestling with conflicting emotions, and went to bed, feeling grateful that the confusing day was over. When I finally fell asleep, I dreamed I was in a garden nursery, looking for forget-me-nots—one of my favorite garden plants. I'd been searching for them for several years, but had been unable to find any before earlier eager buyers swooped them up. In my dream, I spotted several small pots pushed off in a corner. When I investigated, the plants were dried up and scraggly, but with a few sparse blue flowers at the end of the gangly leafless stems. They were not pretty, but I was overjoyed at the discovery! I gathered the droopy little plants into my arms, holding them close to my heart with great joy, knowing certainly that my attention and care would make them thrive and grow and eventually produce the enchanting little blue flowers I adore.

    When I awoke suddenly, I felt curiously impacted by the odd dream. I began to pray, asking God why it should be such an emotional scene for me. That's when I realized its meaning. I was feeling like those forget-me-nots, alone, longing to belong to someone, clinging desperately to life, feeling forgotten and uncared for. But God sees me in my unlovely state and has not forgotten me. He gathers me in His arms, delighting in me, happy to be my loving caretaker, with a plan to restore me to health, wholeness, and fulfillment. Through God's love and tender care, I would revive, not just survive, and would become part of the color and beauty of the world again. And so, as the Bible says, "it came to pass," just as He promised. It always does.

    Thank You for the beautiful garden of all Your tenderly loved children, and that each of us is cherished by You. Thank You, Lord, that even when others may forget us, we are not forgotten by You!

A DOOR OF HOPE

"There I will give her her vineyards and make the Valley of Achor [troubling] to be for her a door of hope and expectation. And she shall sing there and respond as in the days of her youth and as at the time when she came up out of the land of Egypt." Hosea 2:15 (AMP)

The Hebrew meaning of "Achor" is "trouble." What an amazing declaration this is, that the valley of trouble will become a door of hope and expectation because God makes it so. He is a dramatic scene changer. How like God to take something bad and make it good! This is why we followers of Christ should be the most joyful optimistic people on earth. We have a God for whom nothing is impossible, who changes things to such a degree that He is recognized as The Undisputed Champion of All Things!

I am encouraged as I think about historical examples of this. As recorded in the Bible (in Genesis), Joseph was sold into Egyptian slavery by his brothers, was falsely accused and thrown into prison. He lived there for two years, not knowing what would come next. "God was with Joseph," we read, but Joseph didn't have the written record we do, to know that God was with him through it all and planning his release and a grand promotion. Joseph only had his faith. Day by day, he worked at what he was given to do, until he was suddenly released according to God's perfect timetable and placed in a high position of authority to save his family and all of Egypt. "What you meant for evil, God meant for good," Joseph told his treacherous brothers. Their jealousy and anger had forced Joseph to be in Egypt—exactly where God's grand plan for him was preparing to unfold.

It's tempting to doubt God's perfect timetable. Sometimes we are waiting for unseen things that God is putting into place before circumstances can change. Like Joseph, we have no way of knowing what those things must be. Sometimes we are waiting for God to transform our attitudes into more Christlikeness. Either way, it is my job to trust God and live each day doing all things heartily as unto the Lord (Colossians 3:23) while I wait for release from my present difficulty. I can't see the whole picture, but I choose to wait with expectation and confidence for that door of hope to open. The Biblical definition of hope is not wishful thinking. It is confidence in God who loves, saves, and delivers those who place their trust in Him.

Thank You, Lord, for making my valley of trouble a Door of Hope and for opening it wide for me when all things are in place.

"WELL DONE!"

"'Master, you entrusted two talents to me. See, I have gained two more talents.' His master said to him, 'Well done, good and faithful slave. You were faithful with a few things, I will put you in charge of many things; enter into the joy of your master.'" Matthew 25:22-23

Jesus tells a parable about three slaves who were given various sums to invest. The story demonstrates the master's pleasure with the careful investment of what the master chose to distribute to his slaves. I am struck and heart-warmed by the response of the master towards two of the three slaves when they used what they had been given. Given different amounts, both had the same diligence and made their investments count. The master commended them both the same way, although they returned two different amounts to their master. "Well done," he said, and he called them "faithful."

I am counting on this for the time when I meet my Lord in heaven. I'm thankful He does not compare me with the "greats" of the faith. He has entrusted me with certain talents and abilities and only asks me to use them faithfully for what He has called me to do.

We have different callings at different seasons of our lives. Today my body is not as durable as it was twenty years ago, and I live with some limitations I wish were not there. As we age, we are tempted to think our productive days are over. Not so! Although God gives some extraordinary capacity to continue in an active way for all their years, He asks others of us to change direction and develop new avenues of ministry. God doesn't say, "Tsk, tsk, you're done." He inspires us with new ways to serve Him and others, limitations and all! Many older believers in Christ have found dynamic ministries in prayer. Thank God for such a calling! So many of those we call "great" in Christian ministry have clearly credited faithful prayer warriors who undergirded their efforts with fervent and consistent prayers. Encouraging and loving others are also desperately needed ministries in a hurting world. Watch for opportunities to share Jesus' love.

Lord, help us discover Your new ways for us, each and every day. Thank You that You make all things possible, and will give us grace to finish well.

ABOUT THE AUTHOR

Marilee Donivan is certified in "Caring For People God's Way" through the Center for Biblical Counseling. She is a member of the American Association of Christian Counselors and promotes creating art as a valuable aid in bringing healing and comfort to hurting people. The watercolor paintings in this book are her first published abstract and impressionistic paintings. Her favorite painting subject matter is nature and she loves being outdoors to capture its beauty on canvas or watercolor paper. On the facing page is the painting she created by adding details to the cover painting for her book, **FAITH** *Refined*—**Holding On When Life is Falling Apart** (shown below).

Marilee paints, writes, and is a publisher of uplifting books for children and adults.

Her websites are
www.SunriseMountainBooks.com for publishing services
and
www.Sunrisedistrib.com for her art kits and art books.

Some examples:

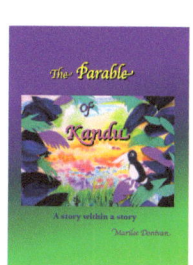
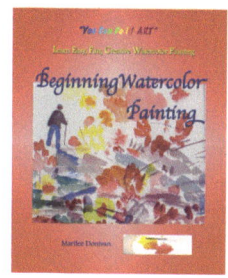
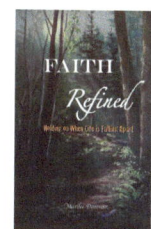

You can contact Marilee Donivan by emailing marilee@sunrisedistrib.com She would love to hear from you and will respond to you personally.

MORE SPRINGS OF HOPE
(Your meditations, quotes, or favorite scriptures. Add them here to personalize your book for yourself or someone else!)

www.ingramcontent.com/pod-product-compliance
Lightning Source LLC
Chambersburg PA
CBHW042123040426
42450CB00002B/51